MEOW

MEOW
MARK BAUMER

Burnside Review Press   Portland, Oregon

MEOW

Cover Design: Susie Steele
Layout: Zach Grow

Printed in the U.S.A.
First Edition, 2019
ISBN: 978-0-9992649-3-5

Burnside Review Press
Portland, Oregon
www.burnsidereview.org

Burnside Review Press titles are available for purchase from the
publisher and Small Press Distribution (www.spdbooks.org).

To Mark, the best son any parents could wish for.
We'll miss you forever.

—Jim and Mary Baumer

One way to introduce this posthumously released book by the beautiful enigma of Mark Baumer is to say something about how, as he lived, Mark was the writer most possessed of freedom—pure, uncompromised creative freedom—that I've probably ever read. By this I mean that the body of work he was able to produce in his heartbreakingly short time on our planet operated rigorously and overflowingly in a matter of vision unbound by convention, expectation, structure, theme, much less awards, credits, recognition; I mean how in everything he ever wrote, whether about vegetables or capitalism, office work or walking barefoot across America, from one word to another absolutely anything might happen, any inanimate entity might find a voice, through any word; to the extent that, from the outside, it seems the work of a child genius, where by child I mean the kind so unaffected by the arbitrary canonical rules that, like Barthelme or Kharms, it seems to describe a version of the world so innately absurd, so blissfully unbound, that many more restricted readers might receive it, one might say, only as might someone looking out through the security grid of our luxury panopticon at a far off and spectacular horizon slowly receding across the wide and darkened land, hearing an old friend's voice somewhere way out there in the receding gradient, saying *it's okay, you will wake up soon, I am here.*

Mark himself might be embarrassed by my attempt at saying this; or, rather, he'd probably just look back blankly at where the words came out and start saying something about food, but then stop himself and be silent. For someone so full of vision, he always carried grace, knew when to let a moment think. Later, in a blog post on any of the countless internet locations where he published and self-published throughout his life, he might write of the experience, "An electric toaster said, 'I believe in freedom,' and then ate so much money it fell into a coma on the longest day of the last new year." That is my poor example of the methods of casual absurdism by which Mark lived his exhaustive ongoing project of unmasking our most flat and blank realities, to reveal beneath the guise of the everyday the unrelenting sprawl of wonder and comic horror that links us all together in a human project no one understands, much less survives.

It's no sort of hyperbole to me that when Mark was hit and killed by a negligent SUV driver in Walton County, Florida, in January 2017, the quotient of America's cumulative emotio-imaginative capability tipped below the holding point of modern stasis we've been living under all our lives. Only those who knew Mark at all could still detect this, despite the countless other warning signs, the sicko headlines streaming by the second through the skin that barely holds our faces together. Suddenly there was no one left to catalog the whereabouts of our *meows*, an intentionally impractical term Mark employs in the short, strange book you're about to read as "a complex mixture of nonvolatile substances of large mass, present in small numbers, along with volatile odor compounds which are small in mass but present in large quantities." It's okay not to have understood that, to have let it wash past you, perhaps to have read it over and again searching for mythic meaning. Like so much of Mark, it's hard to know what to do with the data derived from such supposedly surrealistically intermingled information in the present because it's from the future. It works on paper like a dream, or like a drug (another less than ideal analogy considering Mark was lifelong straight-edge, though also true in how novel language offers temporary psychological change); and still, its essential kernel contains the very sort of empathetic drive that made Mark's work feel at once so random and so alive; by example, it shows one how to see the world and all the strangers in it not as things to be feared, but to be astonished by, over and over, until the fact of existence in and of itself becomes as ridiculous and arbitrary as any trip to Whole Foods, or any corporation's efforts to appear human; or, most of all, as any sentence's desire to predict sense.

In this context, what remains of Mark and in the thankful mass of language his human body has left behind is a display of overwhelming unobstructed *love*, another word we often misplace the meaning of, but herein felt inexplicably in *MEOW*'s shapeshifting narrator's frank descriptions of one's dentist finding "comfort and peace in rubbing his fingers on teeth" while "as soon as one of his hands reaches inside a person's mouth" simultaneously being "able to recall their entire dental history"; love in writing a novel or series or whatever this is that begins, "Hey, it's Bobo, the pregnant meat-eating bear," and then never mentioning Bobo again after that piece; love in challenging one's self to learn to see the world in a way that no one else would have the heart for, even in darkness; in throwing one's self into the impossible, because you can, because what else is life for but such wonder.

—Blake Butler

———

Hey, it's Bobo, the pregnant meat-eating bear. Bobo was only two months old when he got pregnant. He wasn't sure what to do so he did what all Bobos do when they aren't sure what to do. He ate meat. He ate so much meat no one could tell if he was still pregnant. Only Bobo knew if he was pregnant or not. I once asked Bobo if he was still pregnant. He smiled and played me a music song called "I will always be pregnant." This music song became the third most popular song in the world. A lot of people tried to get pregnant so they could be a pregnant Bobo, but it was hopeless. Humans were not capable of being Bobos. A few weeks after Bobo's music song became the third most popular music song, there were a lot of unwanted human babies in the dumpster behind the store where people left unwanted babies. This should probably be sad, but I don't want the story about the pregnant Bobo to be sad, so I decided all the human babies left in the dumpster grew up to be rich and valuable members of their society. One of them was even elected the president of a group of people who run through the forest waving canoe paddles over their heads. Around the same time as all that paddle-waving, the pregnant Bobo began elementary school. He was smarter than all the children because he had two brains inside of him. The teacher didn't think it was fair for the other students that the pregnant Bobo kept winning the math prizes, so on the second day of elementary school Bobo got enrolled in high school where he became the star centerback for the foobowl team and the next day he won the prom crown soaked in pig's blood. Bobo enjoyed his role as the king of the dead pigs and ate a lot of meat to celebrate. His stomach got almost as big as the town where he lived and when he laughed some of the street signs vibrated. The mayor told Bobo he was too pregnant. Bobo didn't listen to the mayor because Bobo was the pig king and also because he was eating meat and Bobo ears don't work when Bobos eat meat. When all the meat in the town was gone Bobo moved to the city and started eating city meat. Bobo was no longer considered the best pregnant blood king in his geographical location, but he was still pretty good and a television studio gave him his own three-hour time segment to do pregnant Bobo things like rub cream on his belly and then rub meat on the belly cream and then eat the creamy meat. This is all Bobo did for a few years, but eventually someone found out he never completed first grade, so the pregnant Bobo got put in jail where he had to throw thinly sliced pickles against a wall all day. No one in jail was allowed to eat meat, so the pregnant Bobo got less and less pregnant until his body was so angry it wrote another music song about not being pregnant anymore. The music song was called "Feed me some more damn meat so I can get pregnant." This song resonated with just about all the non-Bobos in the world and it became the number one song on earth and the jail decided Bobo was rehabilitated and let him out. Bobo was no longer the pregnant Bobo, but he was still Bobo, and he ended up traveling all over the world to eat meat and sing.

———

America is a giant barrel of automobiles running on fumes over a barren wasteland. The soil where I was born was constructed from a pile of melted white penises who once crawled out of a herpes sore named "democracy." Everyone was supposed to bow to this juice hole, but I think we were all too busy looking at the electric wizard standing on his wound ship as the wound ship slowly sunk. And so we never realized we were all going to die unless we learned how to breathe with water in our lungs.

———

I went with my friend to the tattoo lounge where my friend got another tattoo on his face. He said, "I like getting tattoos on my face because it means I'm committed to living life the way I want to live life." His new tattoo was a picture of his girlfriend's face. It was located below a tattoo of his previous girlfriend's face, which was located below a tattoo of a teardrop, which was located below his left eyeball.

—

My dentist never learned to read or write. He doesn't talk much. The only thing he seems good at is putting his hands in other people's mouths. He finds comfort and peace in rubbing his fingers on teeth. There are no patient files in his office. He does not remember anyone's name. But as soon as one of his hands reaches inside a person's mouth, he is able to recall their entire dental history.

———

The owl with large concrete testicles attached to its forehead was not very smart because science recently discovered anything attached to a testicle has a very low IQ.

———

I got an email from Brad today. He seemed excited about some good things. I asked one of my coworkers if he got the email from Brad. He said he didn't like Brad's emails because Brad's emails reminded him of an ex-boyfriend named Gary who used to tell people his name was "Brad." The space heater in one of the other cubicles tipped over and started a small lava mountain. The person who likes to drink four or five diet cokes every day poured some of his diet coke on the small lava mountain. I got worried my email from Brad would get hurt by the small lava mountain, so I threw my computer out the window. It seemed less likely the email from Brad would get hurt after my computer had been tossed out the window, but people in my office were concerned and asked me why I did what I did. I told everyone it was Brad's fault. No one believed me. I tried to call the police because I tend to call the cops in most of my stories, even though I have only ever called the cops once, and it was because there was a weird squirrel trying to touch me in my neighborhood. In this particular story, my telephone didn't work. It was too busy trying to become a part of the human condition. I'm not sure what happened next. My brain was very worried about Brad. It did not seem like there were enough computers in the world to keep Brad safe.

—

Karen and Bill were almost too old to do babies. Both were unsure if they should try. One morning Bill woke up early, shook Karen awake, and said, "Let's do a baby." Karen did not know if this was what she wanted, but she let Bill do a baby to her. Later, when the baby arrived, Bill and Karen were terrified by what Bill had done to Karen.

———

The leaf on the branch would not be a leaf on a branch for very much longer. It looked down at all the leaves who were no longer connected to their branches. They were calm and did not seem to be questioning the purpose of life. Millions of years into the future when all the branches and leaves were gone, the calmness of these leaves would remain. The calmness would always remain.

———

My father was the king of an advanced civilization. His crown was shaped like a color not yet invented on earth. Sometimes he wore a silk robe. Other times he wore a white glove on his left hand. He never wore these two items at the same time. I probably got kicked off my home planet because I set my brother on fire during the festival celebrating his birth. He had been born in the shadow of the love moon, which only existed when the sweat of twenty young virgin boys leaked on the same piece of dirt within the height of the moonbeam's egg development cycle. The ceremony had a lot of trumpets. The king wore his white glove. A lot of happiness teardrops were leaked. I felt very sad and unimportant. My birth festival had consisted of a single twelve-second-trumpet squeak. I had been born under the wrong moon. It wasn't until the trumpets began their fourth hour-long prayer to my new brother that I dropped a handful of candles in the crib. It did not take very long for him to burn. Everyone's happiness teardrops quickly became cold and wet. I did not understand the outrage. What I had done wasn't even that bad. My new brother was not a real flesh system like me or my dad. The government had carved him out of wood. The whole festival was a hoax. No one on my home planet was actually capable of making babies in the shadow of the love moon. In the end, earth turned out to be an okay place.

—

Meowing consists of a combination of genetics, soil, climate, and various production methods. An individual meow is a complex mixture of nonvolatile substances of large mass, present in small numbers, along with volatile odor compounds which are small in mass but present in large quantities.

———

I used to be a large, soft-spoken man who spent most of his life wearing plaid shirts made from submissive colors and fabrics, but all my pores got clogged by the nervous energy my face constantly leaked in my twenties when I only ate bacon donuts because I thought it would be cool to someday get pig cancer in my stomach. Thankfully, the store selling those bacon donuts went out of business and it was replaced by a wooden table so environmentally-balanced and globally-aware-of-itself I decided to only eat twigs of lettuce until my brain got better.

—

Dear bad foods I sometimes eat, I live alone by myself most of the time because I don't want anyone to look at me when I put bad things in my hole, but it often gets lonely and I wish I had a friend whose face was attracted to the same piles of bad foods I am attracted to when I sometimes eat bad foods.

—

The human brain is mostly deficient. Someday I hope to learn how to use my brain, but at the moment the eyeballs in my face are straining under the pressure of all the thoughts in my head. It is impossible to recall everything I have ever seen. I am beginning to forget some of the parts I used to remember. There is a field nearby, but I cannot understand this field because my brain doesn't remember what a field is.

Some elevators climbed inside an elevator especially made for elevators. One of the elevators inside the elevator was afraid of elevators. Someone tried to give this elevator a yellow bean. The elevator began to sweat. All the other elevators were afraid of sweat. They thought it was lava. Some of the elevators climbed the trees inside the elevator to get away from the sweating elevator. Other elevators did not move and let the sweat touch them, but when the sweat touched them they pretended it was lava and their legs got burned off. One of the elevators pretended to be so melted he got turned into marshmallow. All the other elevators took turns toasting this marshmallow on the sweat/lava.

———

I want to write a book that helps people cope with their devastating mental illness because I once knew a person who had to cope with a devastating mental illness, but I'm not sure I know how to write a book that helps people cope with their devastating mental illness, so instead I'll just continue writing this book I am writing.

An old person went back to school to learn how to be a twig. It cost four hundred thousand dollars to learn how to be a twig. The old person believed his life would be better if he learned how to be a twig. On the first day of class, after the professor collected all the money, he told everyone to practice being a twig. None of the people in the class had ever been a twig. They all looked at the professor until the professor made a hand motion that seemed to say, "Get on with it." One person in the class made an awkward attempt at being a twig. For the rest of their time at the twig school everyone tried to copy this initial attempt.

———

The machine I used to create database reports began meowing. Some of the people in my office didn't like it when things meowed. Thinking hard, the office manager tried to turn down the volume on my database reports with a plastic spoon. A guy who knew how to use numbers pretty good was hired to make a presentation about how to eliminate the meowing. His solution was expensive. The meowing slowly became a wrinkle. Two days a week, I tried not to blink. I wore the same dress shirt every day. One of my pant legs had been cut off at the knee. It was easier for the office manager to ignore the wrinkle than it had been to ignore the meowing. At the end of the year he got an award for ignoring the wrinkle. The other people in the office began to whisper loudly at their computer screens. I was worried for the wrinkle. It seemed unlikely it would ever learn how to be a proper un-sexualized crease within the office culture. Some discount cake was purchased. We all dragged our plastic spoons to the conference room. Everyone sang happy birthday to the wrinkle even though it wasn't the wrinkle's birthday. The wrinkle ate cake until it wasn't a wrinkle anymore. We all watched it float away.

———

The object children are fond of touching doesn't exist outside this story. In the story, the object also works as a metaphor for modern culture. People reading this story will probably be reminded of real objects that exist in the world. A few people will stop using some of these objects. The story will be very powerful. Even people who can't read will be influenced by this story. The children are still touching the object. One person reading this story is thinking, "Why do they keep touching that object?!" Every day I get thousands of letters from people demanding I rewrite the story so the children don't have to continue touching the object. It is difficult not to give into these demands. I am not sure what the answer is.

———

The human who made almost thirty-two thousand dollars a year decided to quit his job so he could write a short story. He believed he would be able to sell his short story for two or three million dollars. Before he wrote the story he called the local sheriff and warned the sheriff that he would soon be rich. He also told the sheriff that once he was rich he would stop obeying the law. The local sheriff was nothing more than a wooden broomstick who enjoyed wearing cowboy hats. This broomstick was very good at being a sheriff, but it had recently gotten slightly drunk and could not understand the logic of the man who thought he was going to write a short story worth two or three million dollars.

This is an emotionally uninteresting and deeply unsophisticated narrative about doing bad things with your penises even if you do not own any penises. Before we get started I would like to take a moment to warn everyone not to touch the wrinkle located in the deepest crevice of your pee hole. Also, I apologize for the very white stain I have created by my continued existence.

———

I was at a bookstore. People were soon going to start reading things out loud. I was supposed to read something. My parents were there. The first person who read something out loud talked about themselves for eight minutes before they began reading. I realized I forgot the book I was going to read. I ran home. On the way I decided I needed to buy a wagon. I ran to the office supply store. It only sold sweaters. The snow banks were very large because it was winter. I began running back to the bookstore. It was taking longer than I expected. I held out my thumb hoping someone could give me a ride. A very fast automobile slowed down and crashed into a snow bank. There was minimal damage. I climbed inside the very fast automobile. The driver opened the trunk and installed two flashing lights so other drivers would know he had a passenger. It took a long time to drive where I had to go. It would have been quicker if I continued running. We ended up at my apartment. My roommate, who had been at the reading, was home. I asked him if the reading was over. He nodded and said it ended a few minutes after I left. My life became very worrisome. I began walking down a hallway. Halfway down the hallway, I realized I had never walked down this hallway before. In one of the rooms off the hallway, the driver of the very fast automobile was lying in bed, shirtless, smoking a pipe. I was confused. It was a strange coincidence. The stranger who picked me up happened to live in the same apartment I lived in. How had I not known this?

———

A twenty-three-year-old man named Roger watched a sixty-eight-year-old man kill himself. The sixty-eight-year-old man had decided to kill himself because he could not swallow a piece of medicine without the assistance of a trained specialist. After Roger watched the sixty-eight-year-old man kill himself he vowed that he would also kill himself if he ever got so old that he couldn't do things on his own. Time passed. Roger eventually became a fifty-seven-year-old man. He began having trouble using his own eyeballs. One of them got swollen and the other one only recognized the color yellow. Roger realized it was time to kill himself, but when he tried to do it he ended up crying instead. So Roger continued living until he died the regular kind of death that most people die from when they die from not killing themselves.

———

I wrote this story when I was fifteen. It was the first story I ever wrote. Most of the other kids my age had already written three or four critically-acclaimed-short-story collections. One guy named "Carlos" wrote 117 critically-acclaimed-short-story collections before he was nine. I was jealous of Carlos because his forehead had a full beard and his girlfriend used to date a tenured professor. Carlos didn't like me because I was always asking to borrow his beard so I could go to poetry readings and drink the free wine. I think Carlos used to be my best friend, but I threw a rock at him when we were in "earth science" class. People were always throwing rocks at Carlos. He was pretty good at ignoring the rocks, but the rock I threw wounded his beard and he ran after me until I fell on the ground and broke my collarbone.

———

I need more hugs. It would be nice if I could afford to buy a three-hour hug every twelve hours, but I spent all the money I've ever owned on an object incapable of making hugs. I forgot how emotionally unstable I am when I don't get hugged enough. In the last two weeks I have not gotten any hugs. My life has lost all meaning. I am not sure why I continue to exist. Yesterday, I went to a park and tried to get hugged, but no one wanted to hug a person who is not hugged enough. I even asked a guy with no arms if he could hug me and he made a wet spot in his pants. Then the inside of my pants got sad too.

———

It was puppy night at the ballpark. Fans were encouraged to bring puppies but were not allowed to bring regular dogs. Only puppies were allowed. In honor of puppy night at the ballpark, the home team trained a puppy to play second base. It hit a homerun, but it struggled to make any plays in the field. The home team almost lost by thirty runs. My dad didn't own any puppies. So he dressed me up like a puppy. I was very bad at doing puppy impressions. We were not allowed inside the ballpark. Around the bottom of the ninth, with the home team still trailing by a wide margin, my father and I found a tunnel we thought would lead us into the ballpark, but it ended up leading us deep into the largest wound ever suffered by a human being on a nationally-broadcast syndicated television program. A lot of people yelled at their televisions and told us not to crawl deeper into the wound, but we could not hear them and we continued to crawl deeper and deeper, the whole time thinking we were getting closer to our goal of reaching the inside of the ballpark where the home team was attempting to make a historic comeback which would ultimately fall a half a run short.

———

Two things will either happen in the universe. My friend's new science project will reshape everyone's brain and make every one of us less of an invalid. Or everyone's brain won't ever get reshaped, we will all become more insignificant, and worthlessness will consume everything of quality in everyone's life.

———

I am in the middle of writing three emails to myself. One of the emails is an emotion in the form of some text that doesn't form any coherent thoughts. The other two emails are very sad. They are both currently hanging out at a rundown warehouse someone turned into a dance club. It is two a.m. The emails don't know what happened to their friends. One of the emails accidentally did too many drugs and will eventually pass out. The other email will probably crawl into the draft folder of my email account and never be allowed in anyone else's email account.

——

According to the theory of quantum physics, I am depressed and I will eventually not be depressed anymore because I will be dead, but before I die one of my heartbeats will teach one of my other heartbeats a mathematical theory that doesn't believe in the limits of the human body and these two heartbeats will create a noise capable of vibrating beyond the universe's final heartbeat.

———

The North Pole used to be a guy named "Dan" who lived and worked in a city. Dan's apartment was cramped and sort of smelled like the previous owner's cat. He worked in an office with three or four other people. Everyone genuinely liked Dan, but he had trouble communicating with people emotionally, mostly because he was nothing more than a wandering geographical point whose life struggled to develop a concrete definition of who he was. From time to time he had a tendency to wobble if forced to stand in one place for too long. Then, in the early 16th century, Dan got tired of just being "Dan" and he left the city to become something more than Dan. After a few years of continued struggles, he landed the job that would end up defining how he would be remembered for the remainder of history. Dan. "Dan."

—

On my sixteenth birthday, I lay down in the middle of a highway and didn't move until I was seventeen. For an entire year, automobiles were not allowed to use the highway. A lot of people got mad and said things like, "When I was an adolescent I got circumcised at a gas station." Eventually, I turned seventeen. The part of my emotional development with strong desires to lie on pavement for an extended period of time no longer existed.

———

A man repeatedly dropped his baby on the ground at a sporting event in an attempt to get his face on the large video screen above the field. No one was sure if the man owned the baby or if the baby was someone else's baby. Sometimes the man raised the baby over his head and dropped it. The baby did not seem to mind getting dropped. It did not cry. The baby was a very good baby. The spectators sitting near the man who repeatedly dropped the baby seemed concerned for the baby. Eventually, a stadium official came over and warned the man that if he didn't stop dropping the baby he would be asked to leave the stadium. The man continued to drop the baby. On the large video screen a man eating an ice cream pointed at himself and then held up a single finger to let everyone know he thought he was the best at eating ice cream. The baby-dropping man began to drop the baby harder. And harder. Multiple stadium officials asked the man to leave. He ignored the stadium officials and continued to drop the baby. I'm not sure how to end this. Originally, I thought the baby would turn into something that wasn't a baby, like a plate of nachos, and the man would continue to drop said nachos on the ground. This would make everyone want to chant very loud in one collective voice. Chants of "NACHOS" would fill the stadium. Watching the man drop his nachos, the players on the field would stop playing. The moment would gain more and more cultural significance. Finally, the large video screen would give in and show an image of the man repeatedly dropping his nachos. At this point, everything would get very festive. Fans would throw handfuls of popcorn in the air. Adults would start kissing each other. Children would pretend they were adults. One older man would quietly soil himself out of excitement. And the man repeatedly dropping his nachos would stop dropping his nachos and raise his arms in the air. As the excitement fades, the man sits back down, eats his baby, and enjoys the rest of the game. But I'm not sure.

—

A person went into a bank and calmly said, "Give me all your money." There was no weapon. No threats were made. The person was very polite. Someone gave the person a wrinkled plastic bag filled with money. The wrinkled plastic bag used to be owned by a thick man who liked to rub his thickness on people who weren't thick. Most of the money in the wrinkled bag was crying. The police arrived. There was not very much money left in the bank. One of the bank employees tried to hump a pistol. The wrinkled plastic bag ran away.

———

The first sentence in this story was better than the rest of the sentences in this story because none of the characters introduced after the first sentence had any redeeming qualities and the developing plot had no structure. Plus, the grammatical syntax struggled to maintain its composure beyond the opening line and sometimes it even hurt my teeth to read the other sentences out loud. People who bought this book because they liked the first sentence were disappointed when they got home and found all the other sentences weren't good at being sentences. Most of the reviews of the book said the author was disappointed with his own life, which was why he struggled to maintain the emotional intensity he developed in the opening line. One interesting book review said the author had not felt joy in almost three thousand years. I began to doubt if I would ever write another good sentence ever again. I worried people would remember me as the guy who only wrote one good sentence. Ideally, multiple biographies would be written about my one good sentence and how I never lived up to the overwhelming genius I wasted by only writing one good sentence. Whispers and accusations of drug use and large sexual parties began to circulate. None of these rumors were technically accurate, but a thirteen-year-old high school dropout made a documentary using his dad's video camera, which revealed that my highly touted first sentence wasn't even really that good. This movie went on to win a lot of prestigious awards. The year ended with my agent selling a dirty syringe on the internet, which he said I used to smoke heroin. The judge who bought the syringe made me go to rehab. This consisted of a bunch of celebrity drug addicts building a large, human-sized ant hill in the desert. When I got out of rehab, my agent told me I had to give up writing and I ended up working as an actor in a bunch of made-for-television movies about writers who once wrote books everyone loved but how these writers ultimately had to kill themselves because they forgot how to write books people loved. Everyone seemed impressed at how good I was at pretending to be a depressed author, but the television networks stopped making these types of movies after the most famous newspaper in the world wrote an article about the rise of suicide among middle-school poetry slam contestants. My agent was eventually able to find me a job at a normal cubicle place. Every night, after work, I would come home and make a tray of lasagna. Sometimes I would eat the lasagna, but most of the time I would smear it on my bed and then lay on my bed until it was time to go back to work. My bed turned into a large crusted pile of uneaten lasagna. During this particular emotionally dark period of my life, my mother became worried about my mental sanity. She sent me emails that were loving but mostly nonsensical. One time she sent me an email that only said, "u." I think she meant to write, "Hi. It's your mom. I was just thinking about that sentence you once wrote and how everyone really liked it. Maybe you could write a sequel to that sentence and then everyone would really like you again." I began working on a book tentatively called "The book I wrote that made everyone like me again." It took me a long time to write this book. Maybe like three or four hours. When I was finished I posted it on my secret internet account. No one knew this secret internet account existed. Then I waited for people to start liking me again.

———

The only way to live a complete and full life is if you are elected the president before you are born and then you die in a gunfight a few minutes after the doctor detaches you from the womb.

A few days after gay sex was invented, the majority of husbands in the United States stopped having sex with their male wives and began having sex with each other. This improved the entire mental health of the United States, but the government didn't like people being so happy, so they invented diseases they could blame on the husbands, which would lead to embarrassment and ultimately all the husbands would return to their male wives.

———

In 1962, I went to Hollywood and applied for a job as an American celebrity. One company thought I had potential, but instead of hiring me they shaved my head and sent me to a boarding school for girls. I dropped out of the boarding school for girls and got a job at a fabric manufacturing center where I sewed on buttons for shirts with detachable collars. A few years later I moved to New York City and tried to become an American celebrity again. Most of the people I met thought I was fat and laughed, but these laughs lessened when I started dating this guy who owned his own plane. Vietnam was a popular trend at the time, so I ended up selling the guy's plane to the Vietcong as a practical joke. Some people laughed and thought this would propel me to the fame levels of American celebrity, but most of the senior members in the American government weren't pleased and they did not let me get my American celebrity card. Instead, the United States government impregnated me with three years' worth of children. Even though they were all female, I named each of my children "Jim" after my father. I ended up with four little girls named Jim. With each child I could feel myself growing a little more insane, which seemed to enhance my potential as an aspiring American celebrity. When the last child was out and had learned to walk I went on a major campaign to save the rain forest. I dressed my four daughters up like pandas and made them follow me around wherever I went. The celebrity magazines loved this and some lonely directors in Hollywood began to call. I guess I finally got my break when the mid-seventies rolled around and cocaine became a popular trend. Most of the American celebrities I knew had drug problems and would give up a pile of American money to stop having drug problems. I took on a lot of money and drug problems. At one point I probably had over fifty drug problems. It was okay. My children were still wearing their panda costumes. Things were really great. I even won an award for best actress in 1979 even though I had never been in a movie.

A college student named Phil signed up for a class called "Modern Thoughts," but after the first class he decided he didn't like the professor and dropped the class. One of his friends told him to take a class called "The Nontraditional Beliefs of Things Science Hasn't Discovered Yet" because it was easy. The day of the class Phil overslept. When he woke up he emailed the professor and said he really wanted to take the class, but he had been out of the country for the first two weeks of the semester. The professor told Phil to stop by his office. Phil said he would. The next day a friend sent Phil a funny video and Phil spent the rest of the day watching this video and other funny videos. At around ten p.m. Phil sent the professor an email apologizing for not stopping by his office. Phil told the professor a family member had gotten sick and he had gone home to visit them. After he sent the email, Phil watched a video of a guy puking on his dad who had crawled into a dishwasher. The professor never emailed back. A week passed. Phil sent the professor another email. The professor's email account sent an automated response that said, "I am on sabbatical. My mother is dying. I have moved to the Middle East to satisfy her dying wishes. Please contact my replacement professor if you have any questions." Phil emailed the replacement professor. The replacement professor was an underpaid recent graduate student who had once dated someone who had been at a party where a dad got puked on. The replacement professor told Phil the class was full. Phil began to feel anxious. It was almost the third week of the semester and he was still a class short. He called his father and complained he couldn't get into any of the classes he wanted. His father told him to be a doctor. Phil hung up the phone and went to the cafeteria. He ate fourteen cheeseburgers and then took his own pulse. When he got back to his room he looked at all the available classes listed online. He found one called "Bread is Dumb." The next day he went to the class called

"Bread is Dumb." The professor asked Phil if he had taken any other bread courses. Phil said he didn't know there were other bread courses. The professor said a prerequisite of the class was to have at least taken one other bread course. Phil went back to his dorm and drank a bottle of wine. He then masturbated until his roommate got back from class. Phil did not know what else to do so he put his dick away and lay face down on the floor. His roommate asked Phil if he wanted a cookie. Phil said, "Okay." The next day Phil looked at the available classes again. He saw the class called "Modern Thoughts" was a bread course. He emailed the professor of "Modern Thoughts" and said a computer error had unregistered him from the class. The professor agreed to let Phil in the class as long as Phil completed the required paperwork. Phil went to an administrative building and signed a piece of paper saying he was capable of having a desire to learn. He brought this piece of paper to the professor of "Modern Thoughts." The professor signed the area that said he was capable of being able to make people think the thoughts he told them to think. A few months passed. Phil didn't do any of the assignments for "Modern Thoughts." The professor told Phil he was in danger of failing. Phil asked if there was anything he could do to make up the entire semester's worth of work. The professor told Phil to use a piece of bread to make a cultural statement. Phil photocopied a slice of bread and gave the photocopy of the bread to the professor. The semester ended. Phil got a C-minus in "Modern Thoughts."

I am wood brain. We not brain. On cliff, I thank brain. Wood brain
see free brain coat. Are brain wet? Wood brain pray. Thank you
brain coat. I thank free brain. Should I trade brain or are the
brain stem wet? The brain hair are wood. They are not rocks.
Man brain are free with teen breath. They knew brain wood. Teen
breath spill brain. You are a brain scam. They knew brain flow not
free. The brain flow man spill brain hair on brain wood. I should
trade brain. Thank you wet brain. The hair pray. On brain stem
we thank wood hair. The wood brain knew queer teen. Thank
you spouse brain. Man see free brain on pray stem. Should hair
trade brain cliff? I pray am not man brain. Thank you wood rock.

———

Inside a television mounted on the wall some people did mouth vibrations. It made me realize I was tired of all the noises coming out of everyone's face. Lately, when I open my mouth, I sometimes pause and think, "If I wasn't me would I be upset by the noise I'm about to make?" I can't remember the last time I heard someone make a good noise with their mouth. It's been years. I wish I could sew my ears on something quiet. When people talk I feel my body glaze over after thirty seconds.

———

I wrote a story. It was about a guy named "Neck Pimple." He got dead the same way people get dead if they get dead really bad. I wasn't sure if I should write about dead things, but a piece of my brain touched the other part of my brain and said, "That's a good story. I like when you write good. Dance a little bit until your leg shrivels." I danced for twelve hours. All my legs shriveled. I had to call my third-grade teacher. He had a collection of feathers. Some of them glowed like the kind of money that glows after you take it out of an ATM. My third-grade teacher rubbed his feathers on my legs until the legs floated. I watched my legs float away. It used to be nice having legs. I am just happy I don't have anyone else living in my brain except me. People with other things living in their brains like to smile like bad men. All my smiles are natural-flavored popcorn.

I went to an all-male preschool called "The Academy of Proper Male Babies." All the students wore black turtlenecks so I wore a white tuxedo. When it was crayon time everyone fought over the yellows and oranges. Some children drew pictures of goldfish and suntrout on my white tuxedo. I drew a picture of an octopus. When the teacher hung my white tuxedo on the wall someone stole it. Later, I found it buried in the sandbox. A few years later I married an older man. He was very charming. He took me to three museums before I decided I was ready to get married. Unfortunately, a few days after the wedding he took up a mistress and I was basically alone all the time, but it was not long before something else became interested in me. He took me to a store and I watched him eat. When he was finished I then watched him feed me. We went back to his apartment so we could wash off our crumbs. I spent the next three or four years focused on school. My fourth- grade teacher said I showed promise in my long division. Most of the other children were still wearing black turtlenecks. By this point I had bought another white tuxedo. On the last day of fourth grade someone spray-painted a dead goat's head on the back of the white tuxedo. I wasn't exactly sure what to do but I knew I was physically ready to become whatever gender the world wanted me to become.

———

I got into an above-average but expensive liberal arts college somewhere in New England. On the first night at school I found a box of crayons in my roommate's desk and I ate the green and purple crayons. From that point on, a small boy began following me around on campus. One night when I was in the library I decided I wanted to get my Ph.D. in 18th century literature. My first job after college was as a secretary for an older man. He withheld my paychecks until I started dating him. We got married when the appetizers arrived. After the wedding, I stayed at home with the children even though we didn't have any children. Mostly I cut recipes from cooking magazines and ate them. My doctor said, "Either you're a male wife or you've already developed menopause." I prayed for the second option. A new secretary was hired. He graduated from a prestigious university somewhere in New England. One night my husband said he wanted to have a conversation about my mental ability to raise our non-existent children. The next day a young graduate from a prestigious university somewhere in New England was hired to raise the non-existent children. I got a job living in a nursing home after the divorce. My therapist suggested graduate school. I moved to a part of the country where I wasn't interested in living and spent five years pretending to be productive until someone gave me a piece of paper. I remarried, but before I could remember who I had married my husband joined the army, went to war, and got killed. The next day my therapist died. A week later, my father got an inoperable form of cancer and gave me his hunting rifle. At a job interview I lied and said I had plans for New Year's Eve. Later that night, I found a leftover box of ethnic American cuisine. At around midnight, I pretended some weird guy asked me if I was a scientist. I nodded. He asked if I would be his boyfriend. I shrugged.

———

After the war, I found a place for my loneliness in a six-foot-wide tool shed on the edge of a desert in Arizona. At night, I cooked on a cracked piece of hardware that functioned as a stove. There was no running water. My diet consisted mostly of cilantro and emails I had printed out before the war. Sometimes I would read something my mom had written. Her emails always made me cry. It was difficult to understand how or why I had never written her back.

In 1911, the majority of men in the United States decided against hanging themselves with their own genitals and instead went to work for fast-food restaurants. This decision to not kill themselves had a positive effect on the general population of mainstream husbands. The president of the United States at the time was very happy.

———

Two buddies were standing in an empty field. These two buddies were at an interesting point in their lives. Both of them enjoyed where they were standing. One of the buddies bent down and touched the field. The other buddy nodded and said, "I know buddy." Neither buddy was sure what to do next. The two buddies were aware they were just two buddies, but they were also aware almost every other person in the world was not a buddy. It was almost like the two buddies were no longer part of the world everyone else belonged to. One of the buddies said, "Woah buddy." The other buddy just slowly mumbled something unintelligible. The two buddies were trying hard to just be two buddies. They wanted their entire lives to exist only in whatever present moment they were living. One of the buddies turned to the other buddy and said, "Buddy?" The other buddy said, "Yeah buddy?" The two buddies looked at each other for a long time before one of them turned away and said, "Never mind buddy." A car stopped next to the field. The two buddies climbed into the car and it began moving. One of the buddies said, "Hey buddy, I like your car." The person driving the car looked at the buddy and then at the other buddy. The two buddies smiled. The car slowed down and stopped on the side of the highway. The two buddies climbed out. The car drove away. One of the buddies said, "Buddy?" The other buddy was going to say something but didn't. There was a gas station next to the highway. The two buddies looked at the gas station and waited for it to make a facial expression. One of the buddies sighed and said, "Buddy, I don't think gas stations can make facial expressions." The other buddy nodded and said, "Hey buddy, where are we going?" There was silence. A few minutes passed. It got dark. As the moon began to float into the sky one of the buddies said, "I don't know any more buddy."

—

I ate snowflakes because he thought it would make him better at baseball. When I was six I almost retired from baseball to pursue a career in motorcycles, but my father would not buy me a motorcycle. I spent most of my childhood pretending to be a motorcycle. A few days after my father began having an affair with the entire urban population of Cincinnati, I found a three-inch plastic motorcycle in a dumpster behind a toy store. I tried to ride the motorcycle but it was too small. I put it in his mouth instead. I spent a year of my childhood chewing this motorcycle. My baseball skills struggled to develop while my mouth was busy. I almost found happiness. On the day before I was supposed to join a gang of boys who like to chew motorcycles my brother Ken peed on my three-inch plastic motorcycle. I no longer enjoyed the taste of motorcycles and was not allowed to join the gang. I reluctantly returned to baseball, but sometimes when I struck out I still could taste my brother's urine. I was a baseball player because my dad and brother were baseball players. I didn't really like baseball, but I had a nice swing and people were always telling him I had a nice swing so I played baseball and did pretty good because my swing was nice and baseball was easy. Sometimes I would get bored at baseball games and eat pieces of the baseball field while I thought of an industrial company like "Russia" dropping a nuclear option on America and destroying its ability to enjoy the leisure of baseball. I liked to soak his father's baseball glove in milk during the offseason. Once, I found a pony on my way home from school so I rode the pony to the baseball field. When I got to the baseball field I realized the pony was not a pony. It was a strange man named "Lentil Perez." My father was disappointed in me for letting a strange man carry me. I sat in the corner of the dugout and ate bald crickets. On my twelfth birthday, I went to Kmart with my dad's male wife and my brother Ken. My dad's male wife accidentally parked in the handicap space.

The police were notified. Me, my dad's male wife, and Ken hid from the police in a drain pipe. Ken fed me some pebbles. The cops burned the family car. My father was out of town. After the police left, me, Ken, and my father's male wife had to walk home. That night I watched my father on television. He struck out four times and made an error. In high school, I drew naked pictures of my brother Ken and sold them to major league baseball scouts. One scout from the Baltimore Orioles paid ten dollars for a naked drawing of my brother. After the scout paid for the naked drawing, he put it in his mouth and swallowed. In my seventeenth year of life, my brother's defensive skills improved. I could feel my own defensive abilities shrug indifferently at the idea of improving. During my senior year, I didn't even use a glove and instead wore a rubber goose on his left hand. A week after my brother was drafted by the Seattle Mariners, I pretended I was paralyzed from the waist down. I made a wheelchair out of a tricycle and my father's favorite recliner. When the news leaked, my father dismissed the paralysis as a consequence of massive cocaine use. A few days after my brother hit his first major league homerun, I was waiting for a hamburger at a fast-food restaurant. I told the cashier behind the counter I recently dreamed about eating toilet paper after I used it to wipe my own butt. In a bathroom stall near the house where I grew up someone wrote, "I wish Ken Griffey Jr. was my mom."

I am a feeling of triumph in the human spirit of life. The only way to be beautiful is to be me when I look in the mirror and pretend to be everyone in the world at once. When I am everyone in the world at once I understand what it feels like to feel the best that I've ever felt. If you hear thirty thousand angels meowing from deep inside a mouth filling itself with ice cream then you know what my ears are feeling when I listen to my favorite electronic tingle. I recently met this boy and he looked like he might have been the boy from those movies, which, in fact, he turned out to be. And I said: "oh boy." My face went yellow with smells of gold melted twinkles. While I watched, all the satellites where forgotten movie scenes go to retire turned into a chemical reaction leaking from my other brain. I can't see the future, but I know it's a place about seventy miles west of the best thing I've never touched. When I'm happy I sometimes start smiling so much I can't speak and I just let my chest talk to itself while I listen, admiring how pure and smooth it can hum.

I ran away from home and I'm living with my twenty-six-year-old boyfriend Mark and his roommate Mark. Last night my boyfriend Mark had to work late so I was just sitting on the couch while Mark watched TV. I asked Mark when Mark would be home but he didn't know and kept watching TV. Then the phone rang. It was Mark's boyfriend Mark. Mark picked up the phone and said, "I love you Mark." There was a commercial on the TV. Mark asked Mark a question. Mark said, "I don't know." He continued to watch TV. I didn't like the sound of Mark's voice while he talked to Mark. He sounded like something that had been left in the refrigerator too long. I think it's very difficult for Mark to be Mark because Mark only loves Mark with his penis and he isn't sure what to do with the rest of his body. I started to get ready for bed. Mark, my boyfriend, and I live in a studio apartment so there isn't much privacy. Getting ready for bed means I have to get naked in front of Mark while he says "I love you" to his boyfriend Mark. I got into bed. Mark continued telling his boyfriend, "blah, blah, babe, yeah, I love blah, blah." I got a little frustrated because I had decided to read before bed, but all the words I was reading sounded like "blah blah, I love you too, blah blah." Mark kept touching himself. I gave up reading and decided to watch Mark touch himself. He continued talking on the phone, but he stopped touching himself when he noticed I was watching him. It was boring to watch Mark talk on the phone with his boyfriend so I fell asleep for a little bit, but I woke when Mark was done talking on the phone. He asked if I wanted to turn off the light. I asked him if he wanted me to suck on his penis. Mark was confused. He turned off the light. An hour later, my boyfriend Mark got home. We don't say "I love you" or anything. I just suck on his penis for a little and then he sucks on my penis for a little.

———

The most ideas I've ever done in my life is the time I had a lot of consistent ideas day after day because I found the time, the motivation, and the space to try to make something new in the world like an idea. It probably took me thousands of years to learn this, but I learned it really good until I didn't have to learn anything else. After you've done enough really good learning you can spend most of your free time learning from your own ideas. Even bad ideas that don't have any concept of reality are good at teaching you how to learn a new thing. I've seen other idea people who are more talented and their ideas make the world a better place for ideas, but it is okay for me because the idea arena is not a competitive zone for people to lose and not win. The idea zone is a personal form of optimism that won't stop glowing until all the batteries in your glue cell need to be recharged by expensive island doctors. There are over 180,000 islands on earth. Just yesterday, an idea taught me how to learn that neat fact about islands. I don't mind when my ideas are unoriginal, poorly constructed, and not very talented. A lot of idea people think I have a deficiency, but ideas are not about deficiencies. Ideas are always about the ideas.

My first dog was named "Valley Girl." It had yellow eyes and was good at peeing on couches. One time I accidentally left "Valley Girl" at the beach and she floated to Asia before someone found her and mailed her back to me. I liked to feed "Valley Girl" french fries on the weekend. People were sort of afraid of "Valley Girl" because she wasn't technically a dog. She was an old tennis sock I wore on my left hand when I felt like making dog noises. When "Valley Girl" died I decided not to get another dog. "Valley Girl" was very obedient after she died except sometimes she would try to eat out of a guest's mouth when I had people over for dinner.

—

Yesterday, I woke up at 3:45 a.m. and drank some meows. Then I looked at a book with meows in it. At six a.m. I turned on my meow and opened three meow documents. I looked at these meow documents for about a meow. When it was time to go to meow I put on a meow and went to meow. For eight hours, I did normal meows. At one point, a job applicant gave a meow in the room where meows give meows. He talked about his meows for about a half a meow. After the meow, I went to a store that sold meow, sprouts, and meows. I bought some meow, sprouts, and meows. When I was done, a guy told me he liked a football player named "Meow." It was 6:30 p.m. I looked at my meow for a few minutes. Some other boring meows happened. I was asleep by meow p.m.

———

This book was supposed to be the autobiography of every bear in the world currently suffering from a mental illness, but when I started researching the topic of bear mental illness I noticed bear mental illness was being forced down the throat of almost every consumer demographic, so I gave up writing the autobiography about bear mental illness. Instead I got very depressed. On a lighter note, this was around the time I began wearing a fur hat to work.

ACKNOWLEDGMENTS

Immense gratitude to the family of Mark Baumer for allowing
Burnside Review Press to publish this extraordinary book.

Thanks also to Jeff Alessandrelli for his major editorial efforts and
astounding energy.

"[The object children are fond of touching doesn't exist outside
this story.]," "[According to the theory of quantum physics, I am
depressed…]," and "[The first sentence in this story was better
than the rest of the sentences in this story…]" appeared online at
Poetry Northwest.

Writer, poet, and activist Mark Baumer was the author of *MEOW* (Burnside Review Press, 2019). In 2017, he was struck and killed by an SUV in rural Florida while walking barefoot cross-country to raise awareness of climate change. A graduate of Wheaton College and the Literary Arts MFA Program at Brown University, he was working as a senior library specialist at Brown's Sciences Library at the time of his death. Published in numerous literary magazines, he won the 2015 *Quarterly West* Novella Contest for his novella *Holiday Meat* and the 2015 *Black Warrior Review* Poetry Contest for his poem "b careful." He once wrote 50 books in a single year.